Innervisions

A Collection of Poems

CALVIN DANIEL

ISBN 978-1-0980-0671-6 (paperback)
ISBN 978-1-0980-0672-3 (digital)

Copyright © 2019 by Calvin Daniel

All rights reserved. No part of this publication may be reproduced, distributed, or transmitted in any form or by any means, including photocopying, recording, or other electronic or mechanical methods without the prior written permission of the publisher. For permission requests, solicit the publisher via the address below.

Christian Faith Publishing, Inc.
832 Park Avenue
Meadville, PA 16335
www.christianfaithpublishing.com

Printed in the United States of America

This collection of heartfelt poem
reflect the vision and
goodness of a man who's seen
much, experienced more, and
influenced everyone he's met.

Cal, it was a pleasure creating this
lasting memory
of your experiences voiced in
poetry.

Happy Father's Day to the father
we all yearn for.

Love,
Karen Kohler

Contents

Visions of Nature 7

Visions of Heaven 19

Visions of Life 45

Visions of Friendship 67

Visions of Strength and Courage 75

Visions of Love 87

Visions of Peace 127

Visions of the Past 145

Visions of Nature

Heavenly Design

The heavens so vast so far so wide
Seems endless as I gaze above
The galaxies filled with bright new stars
All created with care and love.

The wondrous light given off by the sun
The roses abloom in the midst of spring.
The rains that fall to quench our thirsts
The melodious sounds when robins sing.

The magnificence to be held by the falling snows.
The wicked seas when tossed by storms.
The gracefulness of the birds in flight.
The mother's love that cheerfully warms.

These wonderful things of which I've spoken
Even the lands where men have trod
Were all designed by that illustrious being
That's known to man on earth as God.

Creation

When God created this old world
He made such beautiful things
The flowers mountains, oceans, seas
As well as human beings.

He placed on earth two lowly beings
To live a life carefree
'Twas thru the sins of those dear ones
That brought existence to you and me.

Man's troubles stemmed from that one day
For the truth has never been hidden
How he was enticed to take a bite
Of the fruits so long forbidden.

Now we must suffer for what he's done
Regardless of the path he's trod
Forever living in the world of sin
Until we return to the hands of God.

Ode to an Eagle

Out in the wild blue yonder
Way high above the earth
Flies the great magnificent eagle
Whose proudness stems from birth
Whether in search of happiness
Or the nourishment it might need
Whether it seeks its loved one
Or food for the young to feed
Soaring along so effortless
With a mind that's ever carefree
Which has always been man's wonder
What is its fate or destiny
'Tis a bird of many a wonder
And forever it will be
An example of god's creations
Endowed with strength and serenity.

Of the Wind

The gentle whispers of the wind
Blows through the Jasmine of my mind
Reaching so deep so far, so endless
Raging onward, never so kind.

Ode to a Waterfall

Out in the flowery courtyard
Stands this lovely waterfall
With rocks that's worn from aging
And trees around so tall.

Its streams are constantly flowing
With waters from heaven above
Just like the ever presence
Of God's undying love.

Its form is so outstanding
There's few that can compare
To the beauty of this waterfall
Whether here or anywhere.

How I love this little work of art
Created from someone's dream
And built with superb perfection
With a form that is so supreme.

The Universe

Who was that architect supreme
Who designed the universe
At which we gaze so endlessly
As things on earth get worse?

Oh what a joy this must have been
To create this maze divine
Where man can stare in joy and awe
And gain a peaceful mind.

It stretches to infinity
And filled with stars unique
Its mysteries are many and untold
Like the Deity we forever seek.

How far it stretches no one knows
'Twill forever to us a mystery be
But its designer and ruler supreme
Is that one almighty deity.

A Lesson to Learn

The sound of music fills the air
The birds so joyfully sing
Of life and love and peace divine
For every earthly being.

They soar along so gracefully
With not a care at all
Their lives are lived so peacefully
Thru winter, spring, and fall.

There seems to be such harmony
In the lives of these sweet birds
I'd dare to say if they could speak
You would never hear unpleasant words.

The lives they live a lesson should be
To all inhabitants of earth
That we should learn to live as one
From the moment of our birth.

Ultimatum

How long will it take a man to attain
That goal he seeks high above
Whether it be for fame or fortune
Or the ultimate of one's true love?

How long must man struggle to reach
That height he has sought so long
One which was failed by many so weak
Yet conquered by few so strong?

Will man ever reach that final goal
'Tis a question one should ask
For to reach that revered ultimatum
Is a most arduous and formidable task.

Unselfishness

There is no end to the good man can achieve
If he cares not for whom the credit is due
He could make this world a better place to live
And unto himself he would be true.

Visions of Heaven

Do Your Best

Care not for what the world may wonder
Only try to do the best you can
Try harder with your each endeavor
To hold on to God's unchanging hand.

A Truth

Despicable is the world's situation
While caring not what others may do
If we added peace, love, and understanding
We just might make some dreams come true

The Ponderer

As I gaze endlessly at the outside world
From the windows of my mind
And ponder thoroughly all the problems
That has long perplexed mankind.

The agony that so long overshadowed
The little known joy and ecstasy
The hate and prejudice so inherent
The lack of peace and harmony.

The absence of love and concern for others
The illegality of deeds performed
Like the battered walls of a deserted fortress
That many a warrior had often stormed.

The problems hence should all our lives
Be a lesson for all on earth to learn
That peace and happiness of so many
Is one which we must ourselves concern.

Inspiration

Through the years we keep on toiling
Thru torrential winds and rain
Struggling onward tirelessly
Sometimes plagued by pain.

Seeking and searching as we go
For the goal we must attain
Maybe the harvest we might lose
Or that fortune we might gain.

Darkened shadows our path might cross
But forward we must go
With heartless beings and those unkind
When none, if ever, does mercy they show.

For we must strive to attain at last
That which we have sought so long
Whether we are those who are so weak
Or those who forever are strong.

Only Beginning

Try as we may in our each endeavor
To sap all the energies stored up by mortal man.
In each our vain and futile attempts
We find that by all the progress
And retrogressive activities
That man has engaged himself in so deeply,
Using fervently those faculties
That were granted by the Supreme Deity
Who rules the entire universe.
Only the mere surface has been scratched
As to the far flung abilities
That man still may find useful.

In Amazement

It never ceases to amaze me
What transpires in the minds of men
The perplexities of a life so deeply etched
The inner feelings they hold within.
The process of thought through which they ponder
The vast universe of which they plan
Trying to solve and sometimes answer
The problems and questions inherent in man.

Sustaining Truths

If in life should any mind wander
Or stray off the course of life as well
Just keep in tune with life's sweet harmony
Make life on earth a heaven, not hell.

Give of yourself that which is worth giving
Never betray a confidence held
Always strive to reach that summit
Live a life with hate dispelled.

Truth and beauty should be your byword
Command respect in love and life
Give total equality also justice
To each your brother so stricken with strife.

Rejoice

Let the sounds of music fill the air
Have all our worries, laid to rest
Let all join in and burdens share
And strive to do our very best.

Let's show the wealth of this great world
By living on earth as one
Quell all our fears so long unfurled
Spread naught but love from dusk to dawn.

Let not the hatred in your heart
Resist the attempt to turn to love
Let all men equally do their part
With strength ascended from heaven above.

Let not the prejudices which we hold
So blindly fill our eyes
To cast from sight our worldly goals
The strengthening of our brotherly ties.

Let not the riches which we hold
So badly mar our self-respect
Less we forget our learnings old
And happiness we do reject.

Let not our ignorance get the best of us
As we show hate for our fellow man
Let oneness thrive in a world like this
As we seek God's unchanging hand.

And Adam Was His Name

When God created Mother Earth
He must have been inspired
He labored so hard for six long days
And rested the seventh for he was tired.

That empty feeling he felt inside
Caused him to make a man
To live and love life to its fullest
And execute his every plan.

God sensed this man's unhappiness
Soon after his life began
And created from a part of him
What he would call woman.

He place her here to comfort man
To share his life and love
To care for him in time of need
With the sincerity of heaven above.

God placed the serpent here as well
Such a vile and wretched thing
Unknown to man its wickedness
Or the sorrows it would bring.

This serpent was the one to cause
The downfall man would make
By enticing him to take a bite
Of forbidden fruits not his to take.

Man's troubles started that fateful day
His life would be quite changed
His world would be a troubled one
Irregardless to how his affairs are arranged.

Utopia

The ultimate of man's one goal
Is to live eternally
Free of sin and all its hands
In peace and harmony.

No more wars, just peace and love
That linger on for years
No more heartaches or emptiness
That's caused by prolonged tears.

Just peace, sweet peace, forevermore
How beautiful it will be
When men on earth can live as one
A life that's ever carefree.

Living Graceful

We should live our lives each day
So it would be a guide for all
Ever so careful of our actions
Walking gently straight and tall.

Displaying a smile upon our face
Whether our minds are troubled or free
Constantly showing our love for others
The way we should so merrily.

Sharing the burdens of our brothers
When they are helpless in distress
Ever conscious of their well-being
Respecting their feelings and happiness.

This would be our life supreme
So unique in every way
If our lives could be so lived
In our living day by day.

The Quest of Man

How long will it take for a man to see
That the way he lives is a sin-
While multitudes sleep without any food
And prisons hold others within.

He tries so hard as best he can
To show the world he loves his brother
Regardless of race, religion, or creed
Whether from one country or another.

Nations still gather in great multitudes
To solve the problems of some
When all we need is peace and harmony
'Til the day our Lord has come.

He should call every man a brother
No matter how few possessions he holds.
He should help his brother who has not-
To accomplish all his goals.

If men from all nations could conform
And live in peace and lasting harmony
We could lay our weapons to a final rest
And let life be lived by all equally.

Inspired Unity

I have often sat in deep meditation
Pondering over the troubles of the world today
How man can sit down at the conference tables
And come to one accord and settle
Some of these major disputes that cause
So much chaos in our daily lives.

How we can distribute those golden harvests
To those foodless beings in the far corners
Of Mother Earth.
We could join hands with other nations
And explore all of those unknowns
That has intimidated man for so long.

Fruitful Labors

Let us strive with each endeavor
As we each seek our happiness
To graduate from roads of regression
To the freeways of success.

Let us set our minds a' working
Free of idleness and malcontent
Let us show with great sincerity
On what our energies we have spent.

Let us seek to reach perfection
From our labors here on earth
Let us live in perfect harmony
From the instance of our birth.

If we took less time for condemnation
And took more time to understand
We could concentrate all our efforts
To improve the lives of our fellow man.

We could clear the house of detention
Give freedom to those who are oppressed
Share with others our abundant riches
Spread love to those so uncarressed.

Let us silence all our weapons
Restore the beauty on land we've trod
Let us lift our voice in praises
To the all-powerful and forgiving God!

Nature in Action

In Flight

Breezing through those silvery linings
Destiny of each unknown
The path they tread is so often trodden
So gracefully, no weakness shown.

Guided by a mysterious vision
Held aloft by precious breath
Carrying the fate of many a person
Many without the fear of death.

So close it seems you are to heaven
Above the earth, the trees and sod
The eyes may gaze in wondrous awe
To try and glimpse the face of God.

The Judgment

Life is so short, so live it full
Through all the hardships of this uphill pull.
Make it so beautiful, so sweet and clean
While living and loving God's every earthly being.
Make it the time to be a success
In lieu of a time for complete idleness.
Hitch your wagon to some distant star
And accomplish your goal Whomever you are.
Praise God Almighty while daily you pray
To lead you and guide you with each passing day.
Set the example for all men to see
That life is worth living the way it should be.
Grow old with grace never with shame
Whether you lived with poverty or fame.
Great your reward in heaven will be
The rest of your days to live peacefully.

Absolute

Warring mongrels filled with envy
Heads of state feel so betrayed
Peace on earth, there never will be
While mercenaries are being paid

Shadows of doom grow close around us
While sinful lives we truly live
Let peace, love, and joy surround us
And enjoy the wonders only God can give.

Slow Down

All too often we pass so fleetingly through life
Flitting aimlessly at such a rapid pace
We tend to overlook the trivialities
That are conducive to meaningful living.

Should we endeavor to abstain from hatred and greed
Reduce our pace and share our wealth (in money, knowledge),
We will find our lives will flourish
With the nutrients vital to everlasting existence.

The Decree

As you enter the corridors of tomorrow
Your yesterdays have now since gone
Success you had in past endeavors
When left uncharted, todays unknown
Set your sights on a far horizon
Chart the course your destiny
Ever progressing never regressing
Attaining your goal with equanimity

Forget Me Not

What can I offer
this cold cruel world
I harbor few riches
and very little fame
I can only offer
my God-given talents
And hope the world
never forget my name.

Visions of Life

Inner Visions

As a child I often dreamed
Just what my future would be.
How I would fare in this old world
And what life would bring to me.

Would I have the freedom of choice
To live my life unique?
Or would I live in constant fear
While freedom I did seek?

Could I live where I made a choice?
Or would that door be closed to me,
By those who choose sustained opposition
While I am striving to be free?

I suddenly awoke to find that dream
Was in fact a reality.
But I will fight with all my strength
To Live my life forever free.

Foresight

All the avenues in our lives
Should be explored very thoroughly
So as to leave no stones unturned
That could jeopardize our being free.

We should strengthen all of our weaknesses
Clear our minds of all debris
Capitalize on all our strong points
And force our weaknesses to flee.

Eureka

Silence is that golden state
In which great men concentrate
Searching for solutions deep in thought
To solve the problems of a world unwrought.

Pondering deeply with each beat
Of the hearts of men that are elite.
Constantly striving for that goal
That great solution for a million fold.

Defeat Sorrow

Life has many unseen sorrows
Which one must overcome
While strolling down life's lonesome highway
And weathering life's raging storm.

Few moments of happiness and much more sorrow
While onward do we trudge
Accepting with grace our loving brother
Whether or not they hold a grudge.

Such is life in each endeavor
Be it fruitful or fruitless
We should strive with all our strength
To make our lives the very best.

The Dream

Try as we may in our each endeavor
To attain the pinnacle of success
The height so far off in a distance
We reach only through much strain and stress.

Live as we may in all our lives
The life unique we strive to live
Go not thru life with hearts so hardened
That we forget what we should give.

Fate

What great secrets does fate hold
As I travel the roads of life
Will mine be filled with happiness
Or plagued forever with trouble and strife.

Damnation

Man is damned by his own virtues
Filled with glory lust and greed
He Aids the progress of so many
Yet there are those he will impede

He controls the fate and destiny
Of many a score of men
He treats one as an enemy
While others as a friend

He retreats with all his riches
As a miser when in flight
He is the deciding factor
In the many battles he will fight

He has compiled tremendous arsenals
With which to destroy his own
Knowing well that he can only reap
A harvest derived from seed he has sown

Man will always look toward heaven
In search of the unknown that great beyond
Until to the call of his creator
He some day will have to respond.

Epitaph of a Success

In this hallowed world of make believe
We live our lives each day
Flitting aimlessly in every direction
In each our own small way

Never caring for the being of others
So overly concerned with ourselves
Blinded by all our earthly treasures
Unaware of those with foodless shelves

Stepping on others as we are climbing
That ladder we call success
Not even showing our inner feelings
Present troubles or happiness

Such is the way we struggle onward
As we live from day to day
Sometimes not growing or possibly caring
While time passes slowly away

Yester Years

The shadows of the yester years
Will linger on and on
Far into years and days to come
When time has passed and years are gone.

Life

Life is a dream
But ever so sweet
'Tis one and one only
A one way street

'Tis a time of sorrow
Happiness and grief
So often with trouble
Without a relief

Endlessly we labor
Each year after year
So often we cry
Never shedding a tear

But such is a lifetime
That is never carefree
Forever and always
'Til life ceases to be

The Trials of Man

In prosperous times men have squandered
The fortunes they have struggled to amass
Some being generous while others held tightly
Not even caring what the die might cast.

Some were philanthropist very unique
Some were misers that hoarded each cent
Some were thoughtful with each endeavor
Some lost it all not knowing where it went.

Such is the way people rush through their lives
Such is the way that some never care
Such is the misery that shadows those who lose
That great mass of wealth which they didn't share.

Such is the story of man and his greed.
Such is the way it will always be
Such are the trials inherent in our lives
That linger on forever through all eternity.

Do Your Thing

When you have done the best you can
And to the world it seems not good enough
Just shrug it off as another experience
And show them all how to strut your stuff.

Time

Time is of no value
If wasted uselessly
In our each endeavor
No matter what it might be.

Time is far too valuable
In our lives we live each day
To sit completely idle
And let it waste away.

Time should have a meaning
No matter who's concerned
To eliminate procrastination
Is a lesson to be learned.

Time is always passing
It waits for no one at all
From the day life has begun
Until death's beckoning call.

Tears I Never Shed

I have often shed many a tear
The most of which I could not hide
To look at me you would not know
The fact that I had never cried

I must have cried from deep within
My feelings sometimes I could hide
Although it seems I may have wept
But no one knows if ever I cried

I shed many tears in times of sadness
Often I shed some tears of pride
'Tis still a wonder and stranger than fiction
How one has wept but never cried.

Unforgettable

What has this world to offer me
If not its riches or its fame
Will it give me, my soul salvation
And then pretend to forget my name.

Remembrance

When those footprints left on earth by man
Are all too soon erased by time
Then all will begin to understand
'Tis better to live a life sublime

Those great reflections cast by man
Would all too soon just cease to be
Like imprints made within the sand
That since has been swept into the sea

The memory of man will live forever
No matter what the die may cast
Until time has past the twelfth of never
And the stars shall fall from the sky so vast.

But how can one forget so soon
That great inhabiter of this earth
Who lived along with life's sweet tune
So gaily from his day of birth.

Footprints Left

The footprints left on earth by men
Whose achievements we know so well
And fruits of labors for years and years
And a story their lives would tell.

How they had foresight so unique
They saw the goal they would achieve
While passing on to fellow men
A philosophy none would believe.

They set their goals on a distant star
Their trials of life were none unique
They had this great determination
A goal they all would seek.

The stories of these once great men
Will live for years and evermore
While men on earth will seek forever
That goal on yonder shore.

Absolutely Not

Man is by far his greatest enemy
His absolute powers make him corrupt
He holds the key to peace forever
That ceases too soon and so abrupt

His exploration of the vast beyond
Are to be held in revered awe
His knowledge is limited to this universe
His future governed by his own law

He holds his own in high esteem
Cares little for the being of others
He treats many as an unfriendly foe
Instead of all as loving brothers

His earthly powers are so minute
While here on earth he daily trod
Cannot compare to those of The Deity
That's known to all of us as God.

Expectations

We live a life of great expectations
Grasping for goals, for fortune and fame
When destinies desired fall short of the finish
We only have ourselves on which to blame.

Visions of Friendship

Harmony in a Dream

In the middle of a beautiful dream
I awoke very suddenly
Only to find to my surprise
It was not a reality

I dreamed that man lived as one
In peace and sweet accord
In lieu of destruction and unpleasantness
With foul and disreputable words

I dreamed that man was free of hatred
For each his fellow man
And vowed to aid a friend in need
In any way he can

I dreamed of love and joy divine
And unity forevermore
Until we reach our destinies
On yonder final shore.

Contemplation

When I'm alone in solitude
I often contemplate
If man could live in harmony
And never deviate

Could he accept his brethren
No matter from whence he comes
Be it the height of society
Or the lowest of the slums

Will he judge one for what they have
And forget he's judging a man
Will he even pause to try and see
If he can lend a hand

Will he step on his fallen brother
While trying to reach the top
Will he continue to wage the wars
That never seem to stop

Will he prepare in days to come
For life in a world beyond
If heaven above is his final home
When to certain death he will respond.

On Friendship

Friendships like a standing tree
A pillar of strength twixt you and me
Such a beautiful life for all to see
Devoid of untruth in a world carefree.

Values

What values should I place on life
My life I'll live my way
I travel the road of which I choose
While living and learning day by day.

Should I place all of my values
On my integrity as a man
Or should I live without even caring
The essence of an unkempt, barren land.

Will I live a life eternal
If values in my life are naught
Will life for me be null and void
As a troubled world so long unwrought?

This decision I must decide
Regardless to what my values will be
My life I live here on this earth
Is one that I must live for me.

Unchained

Control me not for I am capable
Of accomplishing the deeds that must be done
Tell me I can for a nonbeliever
I'll show you when the race I've won.

Visions of Strength and Courage

Unbearable

I find it very, very difficult to maintain
My composure as I sit in deep meditation
Trying so desperately to look interested
Without easing into a most unbearable situation.

On life

What will be our destiny
As we live our lives each day
Traveling down life's lonesome road
In each our own very small way.

Will we seek happiness or despair
Or have no cares at all
Taking life in its golden stride
Unperturbed if misfortune falls.

Will we be of great creations
Or will destruction be our goal
In this world of untold sorrows
Where nature always takes her toll.

We should make this world of ours
A joyous place to live
By learning from our each reception
'Tis such a joy for one to give.

If Only We Could

How often have I sat and wondered
Searching far into the corners of my mind
Why heads of state in this great world
Don't strive harder to unite mankind

Create among man, a common bond
Regardless of race, sex, or creed
Pool their knowledge and their talents
To greatly enhance this cruel world's needs

Use the great tables of discussion
Deploy certain tactics they know so well
Call for arms to be laid to rest
Before the world is a fiery hell

Heed the call of the disadvantaged
Give food to those whose shelves are bare
Show love and compassion for our homeless
Our hoards of wealth we all could share

Make the goal of every nation
One we all will strive to attain
Live on earth in one accord
And never from peace do we refrain.

The Question

What truth is there in any man's word
If that word is not his bond?
What life will he have to live forever
When he passes on to that great beyond?

Will he have a fruitful life
Or will his life be one that is damned?
Will he have attained any knowledge of matters
For which on earth many years he crammed?

Will his hard labor be rewarded
Or will it go forever unsung
Like those before so handsomely rewarded
While climbing the ladder rung by rung?

No one can say how mans life will be
Or how he will fare when he departs
Whether it is fruitful or serene
It all depends on how he starts.

The Uncommon Man

How do we thank the uncommon man
The one who struggle for years
Who takes an idea and makes a success
While overcoming many of his fears

He makes his dream a reality
His integrity is unquestionably true
His glory and honors nonexistent
That are all too rare and long overdue

Oblivious to all trivialities around him
Trudging forward down life's byways
Like a bird in flight, very carefree
Uncaring of the world's unsightly haze

Give honor to this wonderful being
Who will execute a well-thought plan
Let it be known to all the world
That here exists that uncommon man.

On Being Free

Where are those faithful patriots
Who live and breathe democracy
The ones who fight with unfaltering strength
To preserve our rights to being free
Are they themselves so deeply engrossed
With trivialities that gain them naught
Why don't they give this country freely
The full support they should and ought

Greatness

The greatness achieved by any one man
'Twas not on his merit alone
But through hard work and difficult times
Far into the night when the day was gone
Endlessly laboring it would seem
To achieve that final goal
Constantly carrying and often sharing
The burdens of life untold
Finally achieving that goal at last
The dream so close at hand
So many attempt but so few attain
That greatness sought by man

Shadows

Shadows of your loveliness
Lurk deep within my mind
Shadows of the one true love
Whom once I left behind

Shadows of your gracefulness
In every step you take
Shadows of the rendezvous
We often tried to make

Shadows of your happiness
Which we will never share
Shadows of the soft words spoken
With tender loving care

Shadows of the love we knew
In our first and last endeavor
Shadows of your smile so sweet
That now is lost forever.

Ode to the Far Easterners

We take this time to salute our compatriots
Whose roots stem from the great Far East
Whose contributions to this society
Sometimes the difference between famine and feast
Who served so diligently when called to arms
Who performed the tasks desired by few
Who struggled on with each endeavor
To adjust to a life to them so new
They blended in this land of ours
And soon we were all one family
We welcome them with open arms
To live forever in harmony.

Unchain Me

Hinder me not
for I am capable
of accomplishing the deeds
I wish so done

Give me a chance
I am an achiever
I'll show you when
the race I've won

Visions of Love

Gone

Gone are the heartaches that lurked deep within
Gone are the times that we once knew
Gone are the moments that we once shared
Gone is the love that once was true.

Gone is the happiness once so divine
Gone are the rendezvous we tried to make
Gone are the words so softly spoken
Gone is the music of the world we did forsake

Never

Forsake me not
when I so need you
Despise me not
when I do care
Share with me
All days so lonely
Our hearts are love
And not despair

Earth Angel

The elegance of her sweet perfume
Still lingers in the air
Floating about a dimly lit room
With traces in her hair.

The Gentleness of her sweet soft voice
Can be felt all pleasingly
To love her you would have no choice
For she never loves teasingly.

Her beauty is one you must behold
There's none that can compare
Not even the dreams so often told
Whether here or anywhere.

Her silky skin is soft and sweet
Her eyes are such a dream
One without grace could never compare
Her magnificence is too supreme.

For she is one a man could love
From now throughout eternity
She descended to earth from heaven above
To be my fate and destiny

Learning to Keep Her

The things you did to win her over
You must continue to make her stay
Ever so mindful of matters important
In your each endeavor day by day

Continue the kindness you displayed
When you were trying to win her hand
Showing the goodness she thought you had
When she chose you to be her man

Give her flowers regardless of the occasion
Tell her daily of the love you share
Stroke her gently with deep affection
Make her know that none compares

These small things are most important
Regardless to what anyone will say
Whatever you did to win her over
You must continue to make her stay.

Love Expressed

I need you like
the flowers need rain I hear your every step you take
I breathe the very
air you are breathing I love you girl
for goodness sake

Mystery Woman

You are the sweetness of many a dream
You control each breath I take
You are just as lovely as you seem.
If I am asleep don't let me wake
My love for you Is oh so strong
You brighten up My days
My life, my love please carry along
I love you in so many ways.

Dream Girl

I have traveled this whole wide world
In search of a love this new
This I can say from my heart
I've never seen a girl like you.

I traveled to New York in the summer
To lovely Rome so covered with dew
To Monaco where the tides come in
But I've never seen a girl like you.

Oh, what a maze the constellation
That's filled with stars above
Oh what a thrill when you are near me
I am filled completely with love.

I may climb to the top of the mountains
And dream of happiness we once knew
Search the heavens and earth forever
But I'll never find a girl like you.

True Beauty

Elegance is just one of your virtues
Your loveliness cannot be compared
Beauty and charm is yours forever
Love like ours is never shared.

Ode to My Love (Valerie)

Visions of success lurks deep within
A lady of wisdom of strength and love
Loveliness in her to be compared
Ever the essence a righteous dove.
Roses in bloom could be no sweeter
Inside an endlessly Beauty,
Endowed from above.

How Is Love?

How do I love thee, my precious?
More than any words can say
Deeper than the deepest ocean
Brighter than the sunniest day.

Stronger than the strength of thousands
Wider than the whole universe
Softer and sweeter for the better
And graciously soothing for the worse.

I love thee, my love so endless
Like the vastness of the heavens above
My feelings run as deep and endless
Like the essence of a mother's true love.

How, my dear, do I love thee
I love thee in so many ways
My love for you is everlasting
And true for the rest of my days.

Still Waters

Your waves are smooth and high
As you bring to the surface
Your love of responsibility
And completion through
Full communications
And acknowledgements.

I love you.

Your new year
Is the manifestation
Of the best within you.

The Exit

This is our final salutation
With great sadness we will depart.
Searching the horizon here and yonder
In search of love lost from our heart.

Be Mine

A starless sky so high above
The wind does chill the air
'Tis time to hold the ones we love
With tender loving care.

We care not what the future brings
We live our lives each day
So high above the birds will sing
As they go on their way.

A gentle nook where lovers hide
With peace and love supreme
Just like the rushing of the tide
In a dreamer's golden dreams.

The wondrous joy of love to share
With one whose hearts so kind
Just stroke so gently her soft hair
And say be my Valentine.

Love Is

Love is making one happy
When he or she is sad
Love is the greatest feeling
That one has ever had

Love is far too beautiful
To be marred with any hate
Love is that constant feeling
That should never deviate

Love is loving each other
With tender loving care
Love is the simple caressing
The strands of a loved one's hair

Love is making things easy
For the two it may concern
Love is a beautiful lesson
That all should strive to learn

Love is constantly caring
For all your loved one's needs
Love is helping them progress
And never to impede

Love is being so gentle
In things we do or say
Love is loving each other
In a most enjoyable way

Love is being so thoughtful
Of things that must be done
Love is forever pursuing
Until that love is won

Love is a happy feeling
Through all of its endeavors
Love is that beautiful thing
That should last and last forever.

Searching for Love

Oh, I have traveled far and near
In search of dreams that didn't come true.
From sea to sea and shore to shore
And the vast horizons far so blue.

I have climbed the highest mountains
Braved the fiercest of storms
Searching far, so near, and yonder
For that love that gently warms.

When I have found that love so truly
My travels then will cease to be.
I'll spend my life in love while sharing
The love I have, and her love for me.

A Mother's Love

The world may hold eternal richness
The skies seem endless high above
The love that man shows for each other
Cannot compare to a mother's love.

The stars may shine as bright as day
The clouds may fill the skies above
The strength that's found in the arms of many
Will never be as strong as a mother's love.

The trees that stand in yonder forest
Are blessed with rains from up above
Their roots are deep and seem so endless
But never so profound as a mother's love.

We speak of riches, stars and trees
The most wonderful thing anyone can say
Is, I Love you, Mom, and thanks to God
For my dear mother on this Mother's Day.

Content

Happy are we on this occasion
Smiling gaily content at heart
Love abounds where we enter
The way it did right from the start.

Of Lovers

Distance creates such sorrow
Between two lovers hearts
Strength and sheer determination
Will never let them part.

Eleganza

Her loveliness can be compared
To a rose in fullest bloom
Like stars above so heavenly
Her radiance relieves your gloom.

Her elegance is so unique
There's none that can compare
Her smile is one you cannot find
On earth or anywhere.

Her lips are sweet like cherry wine
Her perfume soft and sweet
To see her walk so graciously
Is a most delightful treat.

Her lips are like a starlit night
A sweetness one would proudly share
Her magnificence is further graced
By silken strands of wavy hair.

Her perfume is the radiance
Of a garden filled with dew
With that captivating essence
That tends to capture you.

Her creamy skin is so divine
So gentle to the touch
Her love is one that is so unique
That one would desire so much.

Her voice is sweet like violins
She gives life to my soul
She means the whole wide world to me
Such a lovely lass to behold.

A smile from her lightens my heart
It brightens up my day
No man could help but loving her
In a most delightful way.

She is the world to a lucky man
The answer to a poor man's prayer
She loves so deep and endlessly
With grace and loving care.

Sweet Eleganza you are a dream
How wonderful you are
Like ripples on a rushing brook
That flows beneath a distant star.

For she's a girl any man will love
Her goal is not for fame
Because her love's an undying ember
And Eleganza is her name.

Internal Beauty

Just as beautiful as a summer rose
Inside a heart of solid gold
Like the brightness of the morning sun
Life to her is beautiful like the goodness in her soul.

Happiness is just one of her virtues
Ever the one to seek her goal
Lasting friendship could be her motto
Enriched with loveliness like a dream untold.

New spring is she in her life lived daily
Endlessly giving life her all
Interminable is she in getting the job done
Down-to-earth to neither stumble of fall.

Love Fleeting

Feelings are
Just few moments
To be shared
By a happy two.

Love can enter
And quickly exit
Never knowing
A dream come true.

Icy Fingers

Your icy fingers squeeze my heart
Yet still I feel so deep and warm
You toy so endless with my emotions
When you invariably turn on the charm.

My Love for You

I could fill a cornucopia
With roses soft from dew
And spread them after your every step
To show my love for you.

I will fill the clouds so high above
With April showers we once knew
And sprinkle them gently all around
To show my love for you.

I will search the heavens for a star
That shines so bright like new
And cast its light upon your face
To show my love for you.

I will build a castle from the sand
And color it midnight blue
Place diamonds and gems on every wall
To show my love for you.

For I am one who loves not weakly
But one that loves so true
I'd travel to the ends of Mother Earth
To show my love for you.

Dream

Dream, my love, a golden dream
'Til your heart is filled with glee
Dream, my love, a wondrous dream
Dream, my love, just dream of me.

Dream, my love, a splendid dream
Just like the ones we used to share
Dream, my love, a simple dream
Of winds blowing gently in your hair.

Dream, my love, a beautiful dream
Where the stars will gently sing
Dream, my love, a fancy dream
Where you imagine me a king.

Dream, my love, a lovely dream
Until our hearts shall blend
Dream, my love, of heartaches gone
That now are blowing free in the wind.

Weep No More

Weep no more, my fair lady
The worst is yet to come
The battle is near, the air is filled
With rockets, mortars, and bombs

Men are dying all around us
But onward we must go
There is no mercy here at all
Whether neutral, friend, or foe

At last we reach our final goal
Let the horn of triumph sound
Weep no more my fair lady
For I am homeward bound.

The Flight of a Butterfly

Cage not the butterfly of love
Let it fly ever so free
Should it fly away and never return
'Tis a love not meant to be.

Should it fly away and soon return
To the nest it had forsaken
Accept it graciously with open arms
For true love is never mistaken.

Show it love and care so genuine
With hope each passing day
That the need to fly and never return
Shows a fancy that has passed away.

Blooming Beauty

Each day in life you grow much lovelier
Life to you more than a song
Inside a beauty that is so unique
Zestful and happy as the days are long.

A lady of strength, of wisdom, and character
Beautiful as a rose in bloom
Endlessly loving, caring, and giving
'Tis like soft light in a dimly lit room.
Happiness abound, not a trace of gloom.

To Mother

How do I thank her for all she's done?
In a life with troubles like mine
Endlessly loving, working, and giving
With a heart that's' far too kind.

Constantly teaching me from birth
Until this present time
That its better to live in poverty
Than live a life of crime.

Sometimes alone and she would cry
When we often went astray
But she never stopped loving us at all
Until this present day.

I'll always thank her and love her too
For there could be no other
Because her love's an eternal love
Thank God for my dear Mother!

Cupid's Holiday

Once a year we have this day
To tell the one we love
How much they really mean to us
With the sincerity of Heaven above.

We shower them with gifts and love
To show them that we care
We tell them that we love them so
And their love we will always share.

We hold them dearest to our heart
As years pass on and on
We love them deep and endlessly
And more when they are gone.

The feeling there will forever be
No matter what the sign
So hold her near and close to you
And say, Be my Valentine!

Love's Course

Think not you can guide the course of love
Found worthy love will guide your course for you
Harden not your heart when love will call
Let love abide and to thyself be true.

The Verge of Happiness

When one is on that beautiful verge
Of the garden of happiness
One seeks to find and hold so near
That one that shared the strains and stress.

The one that shared the heavy burdens
That one encountered along the way
The one that made those burdens lighter
As one went through life day by day.

The one who made the pulse of life
Beat sweeter with each beat
The one whose love for one was strong
So filled with joy and so complete.

The one whose heart was filled with love
As one lived day by day
The one who found that long last happiness
As they went on their way.

Ode to Fathers

Father is the one who wins
The bread his family needs
Totally responsible for their welfare
Their behavior and their deeds.

He works so hard each live long day
And far into the night
To give his family all the comforts
That make their lives so bright.

He must be the judge and counselor too
As well as other things
He is the one who must decide
Their future lives and the joy it brings.

For he is one we all should love
In each our own little way
And say with joy and love divine
We love you, Father, this Father's Day.

Mothers Are

Mothers are those beautiful pillars
That support the world of love
Endowed with grace and honesty
That's sent from heaven above.

Mothers are those towers of strength
That hold the ties that bind
Unique in each their own small way
With hearts that are so kind.

Mothers are those wonderful beings
Whose hands will guide her young
To the top of the ladder of success
From the lowest of the rungs.

Mothers are those who always care
They soothe our troubles away
So we would like to take this time
To say thank you, Mother, this Mother's Day.

Happy Twelfth Anniversary, Honey

There was no card that I could find
That could better express my love
For you, my sweets, forevermore
As prescribed from up above.

When we first met in 1980
You said I would be your man
The plan you crafted so perfectly
Worked where I would take your hand.

I've been so happy through all these years
You wouldn't believe how much
I've become accustomed to your feelings
Your warmness and your touch.

The little things that I would do
To cause you such dreadful pain
Were done without any thought or reason
Without realizing I had naught to gain.

Oh, yes, you came into my life
You changed me when you could
Your sweetness always ever present
Your intuition being ever so good.

You are always right and seldom wrong
I could never ask for more
A woman like you are one in a a million
On earth or the celestial shore.

I don't always say I love you
As often as I should
But, honey, you know me through and through
To you I will ever be good.

No matter what the future brings
You will forever be my number one
My love, my friend, and best critic
One whom I may share laughter and dance and have fun.

This poem is really special
For that special person in my life
The one who means the world to me
My very special, loving wife

So here's to you straight from the heart
I will make your dreams come true
Wishing you happiness and tons of love
And a very special 12th anniversary Just for you.

Eternity

When I have reached my journey's end
And life has ceased to be
Bury me not on land my friend
But down in the deep blue sea

There I can mingle with the waves
And all the life therein
Until the world is free of slaves
And there is no more sin

Deep within the icy blue
An eternity I will spend
Until injustices on land are through
And there's a oneness in all men.

Visions of Peace

The Goal

No matter what
the world surrenders
We all must strive
to live in peace
Let happiness thrive
here deep among us
And harmony abide
and never cease.

In a Wonder

How can I live
a life of peace
If this cold world
won't let me be
Perhaps I can etch
a meager existence
And try my best
to forever stay free.

Visions

The world could have a lasting peace
If we lived a life sublime
The endless wars would even cease
In a matter of some time

We could live in brotherhood
With love and joy divine
No more bad but only good
From a oneness in mankind

Prosperous men would all derive
The fruits of a world unique
Whether it's happiness for which they strive
Or the prosperity they might seek

Forever beauty should this we attain
In a world so filled with hate
Only rejoicing and no more pain
If such could be our fate.

Selfishness

The progress man achieves is all too endless
If he cares not for whom the credit is due
He could make this world a better place to live
And unto himself, he would be true.

Second Chances

The cruelties and anguish life possess
Are those of pity and prejudice
Somehow one must contemplate
The unjust treatment of Mother Earth.
For the south is the center of all life and birth.

Take a moment, what it's worth
For man to treat man so unkindly
Give life a second chance
A chance that exist only in those who believe in dreams
For there is no life without a second chance
That life of dreams only men can dream.

Endurance

Life has many unseen difficulties
Which one must overcome
While strolling down that lonesome highway
And weathering the raging storm.

Few moments of happiness and much more sorrow
While onward we do trudge
Accepting with grace our loving brethren
Whether or not they hold a grudge

Such is life in each endeavor
Be it fruitful or fruitless
One should strive with all his energies
To make this life the very best.

Imagination

The world could have a lasting peace
If we lived a life sublime
The endless wars would even cease
In a matter of some time.

We could live in brotherhood
With love and joy divine
No more bad but only good
From a oneness of mankind.

Prosperous nations would all derive
The fruits of a world unique
Whether it's happiness for which they strive
Or the prosperity they might seek.

Forever beauty should this we attain
In a world so filled with hate
Only rejoicing and no more pain
If this could be our fate.

Connected

The earth and its perfection
Is the reflection
Of one's inner peace
And integrity…

For the world is beautiful…
There is nothing to search for…
Nothing to find.

You take you everywhere.

Essence of a dove

I feel the strength of millions
As I live my life each day
I see the stars that few men see
Whole passing along the way.

I feel the warmth of billions
As I sow peace and love
By living life so freely
As the essence of a dove.

A Mirage of Peace

When man has laid his weapons down
To lift them up no more
There will be an everlasting peace
On earth from shore to shore

The hatred for his brethren
Will soon subside to nil
If peace will be his final goal
When made of his own free will

The world could sing sweet praises of
Much love and joy divine
And brotherly love would long exist
In this world of yours and mine

All men should strive for peace, sweet peace
And love and joy forevermore
Until we all will gather as one
On that great and golden celestial shore.

Why Not Care

Could you care less if the world existed
Could you show care when there's no peace
Would you hold man in high esteem
While he holds life on a short-term lease.

That Blessed Holiday

Every year about this time
The air is filled with cheer
We take this time to celebrate
When Christmas Day is here.

We shower all with gifts of love
At home and far away
For we are thankful for all it all
On that blessed holiday.

We give our praises to God above
For the blessings he did bring
Toward peace on earth unto all men
By letting freedom ring.

We decorate our homes so sweet
With love and joy divine
We find it hard for anyone
To have a word unkind.

We celebrate the birth of Christ
Our Savior and our King
While high above our earthly home
The angels sweetly sing.

We fill our tables with sweet joy
We share with one and all
The gifts of love we give so freely
Whether they be big or small.

This is a happy time in life
A million words couldn't say
Just how we feel so full of cheer
On that precious Christmas Day.

We hope with all sincerity
To those who heed our call
That this will be a very happy
And Merry Christmas to us all.

The Decision

No matter what the world surrenders
We all must strive to live in peace
Let happiness live here deep among us
And harmony exist and never cease.

Daring St. Nick 2

We dare St. Nick to pass our place
Without stopping by to say
A hearty hello to all our folks
In a most enjoyable way.

We dare St. Nick to fill his sack
With naught therein for us
Without him having one heck of a time
From our making such a big fuss.

Reflections

Have we done our share today
To make a world of peace
Have we shown someone we care
Or I love you to say the least

Did we stop to share our fortunes
With those of us with naught
Did we greet our fellow man
The way we should and ought

Can we live with all our riches
And keep them to ourselves
Can we ignore the poor and hungry
So plagued with foodless shelves

If we can answer these truthfully
With a simple answer, yes or no
And learn to share with each our bounties
While down the road of life we go.

Visions of the Past

My Departure

I say this to you on my departure
With deep regrets, you I must leave
Carry on with each your own endeavor
Let us trudge onward never to grieve.

You have a mission most important
To be benefited by more than you'll ever know.
Those serving us so proudly stateside
And those abroad on a distant shore.

Sometimes no light shines from the tunnel
But forever forward you must go
Ever mindful of each your teachings
Stressing the points the troops should know.

The job may seem now not rewarding
But stick with it until the end
I leave you now but not forever
For deep in my heart you are ever a friend.

The Nurse

She seems so very cheerful
As she goes about her work
Constantly caring for patients
Whom she will never shirk.

Her efforts seem untiring
As she goes on and on
Forever seeking and checking
From darkness until dawn.

Her efforts go unheralded
With each new passing day
Filled with warmth and passion
As she goes on her way.

Words alone are insufficient
For there could be no verse
That could quote the many honors
That's due a pleasant nurse.

Ode to the New Room

It sits there with its wall of brown
And floor that's nice and green
Its seats are round of red and yellow
And windows sparkling clean.

Its ceiling is so white and pure
Laid out with man's own grace
Where people stop to drink and eat
As they talk face to face.

Its tables are a work of art
That only a master could groom
It's the new addition to our place
We call our little bar room.

Ode to a Guitar

The melodious sounds of a sweet guitar
Makes my heart beat rhythmically in tune
Like the flowing of a mountainous stream
And the gentle chirps of a bird in June.

Its lines are sleek and filled with grace
Created by the skill of a master's hands
It's soft, sweet tunes are heard for years
In many a foreign and distant land.

Its strings are strong and so unique
The sounds they make when strummed
Are like the sounds of a heavenly choir
And of a million sweet words so sweetly hummed.

It makes the heart of many a lover
Fill rapidly with joy and love
It makes the sound so rich and sweet
Like a band of angels from heaven above.

This work of art is too magnificent
To ever be destroyed or marred by man
Its loveliness will live forever
Just like that touch of a master's hand.

Daring St. Nick

We dare St. Nick to steer his sleigh
While Rudolph with a nose so red
Leads all the reindeer through the night
While towing Santa's toy-filled sled.

We dare St. Nick to stop by here
While he is on the way
Because we'd like to wish him truly
A most happy and joyous Christmas Day.

Innervisions		
Poem Titles	**Page**	**Topic**
Absolute	41	Visions of Heaven
Absolutely Not	64	Visions of Life
A Lesson to Learn	15	Visions of Nature
A Mirage of Peace	138	Visions of Peace
A Mother's Love	105	Visions of Love
And Adam Was His Name	30–31	Visions of Heaven
A Truth	22	Visions of Heaven
Be Mine	101	Visions of Love
Blooming Beauty	117	Visions of Love
Connected	136	Visions of Peace
Contemplation	70	Visions of Friendship
Content	106	Visions of Love
Creation	10	Visions of Nature
Cupid's Holiday	119	Visions of Love
Damnation	53	Visions of Life
Daring St. Nick	151	Visions of the Past
Daring St. Nick 2	143	Visions of Peace
Defeat Sorrow	50	Visions of Life
Do Your Best	21	Visions of Heaven
Do Your Thing	58	Visions of Life
Dream	114	Visions of Love
Dream Girl	95	Visions of Love
Earth Angel	91	Visions of Love
Eleganza	108–109	Visions of Love
Endurance	134	Visions of Peace
Epitaph of a Success	54	Visions of Life
Essence of a dove	137	Visions of Peace
Eternity	126	Visions of Love

Innervisions		
Poem Titles	**Page**	**Topic**
Eureka	49	Visions of Life
Expectations	65	Visions of Life
Fate	52	Visions of Life
Footprints Left	63	Visions of Life
Foresight	48	Visions of Life
Forget Me Not	44	Visions of Heaven
Fruitful Labors	36–37	Visions of Heaven
Gone	89	Visions of Love
Greatness	83	Visions of Strength and Courage
Happy Twelfth Anniversary, Honey	124–125	Visions of Love
Harmony in a Dream	69	Visions of Friendship
Heavenly Design	9	Visions of Nature
How Is Love?	98	Visions of Love
Icy Fingers	112	Visions of Love
If Only We Could	79	Visions of Strength and Courage
Imagination	135	Visions of Peace
In Amazement	26	Visions of Heaven
In a Wonder	130	Visions of Peace
In Flight	39	Visions of Heaven
Inner Visions	47	Visions of Life
Inspiration	24	Visions of Heaven
Inspired Unity	35	Visions of Heaven
Internal Beauty	110	Visions of Love
Learning to Keep Her	92	Visions of Love
Life	56	Visions of Life
Living Graceful	33	Visions of Heaven
Love Expressed	93	Visions of Love
Love Fleeting	111	Visions of Love

Innervisions		
Poem Titles	**Page**	**Topic**
Love Is	102–103	Visions of Love
Love's Course	120	Visions of Love
Mothers Are	123	Visions of Love
My Departure	147	Visions of the Past
My Love for You	113	Visions of Love
Mystery Woman	94	Visions of Love
Never	90	Visions of Love
Ode to a Guitar	150	Visions of the Past
Ode to an Eagle	11	Visions of Nature
Ode to a Waterfall	13	Visions of Nature
Ode to Fathers	122	Visions of Love
Ode to My Love (Valerie)	97	Visions of Love
Ode to the Far Easterners	85	Visions of Strength and Courage
Ode to the New Room	149	Visions of the Past
Of Lovers	107	Visions of Love
Of the Wind	12	Visions of Nature
On Being Free	82	Visions of Strength and Courage
On Friendship	71	Visions of Friendship
On life	78	Visions of Strength and Courage
Only Beginning	25	Visions of Heaven
Reflections	144	Visions of Peace
Rejoice	28–29	Visions of Heaven
Remembrance	62	Visions of Life
Searching for Love	104	Visions of Love
Second Chances	133	Visions of Peace
Selfishness	132	Visions of Peace

Innervisions		
Poem Titles	**Page**	**Topic**
Shadows	84	Visions of Strength and Courage
Slow Down	42	Visions of Heaven
Still Waters	99	Visions of Love
Sustaining Truths	27	Visions of Heaven
Tears I Never Shed	60	Visions of Life
That Blessed Holiday	140–141	Visions of Peace
The Decision	142	Visions of Peace
The Decree	43	Visions of Heaven
The Dream	51	Visions of Life
The Exit	100	Visions of Love
The Flight of a Butterfly	116	Visions of Love
The Goal	129	Visions of Peace
The Judgment	40	Visions of Heaven
The Nurse	148	Visions of the Past
The Ponderer	23	Visions of Heaven
The Question	80	Visions of Strength and Courage
The Quest of Man	34	Visions of Heaven
The Trials of Man	57	Visions of Life
The Uncommon Man	81	Visions of Strength and Courage
The Universe	14	Visions of Nature
The Verge of Happiness	121	Visions of Love
Time	59	Visions of Life
To Mother	118	Visions of Love
True Beauty	96	Visions of Love
Ultimatum	16	Visions of Nature
Unbearable	77	Visions of Strength and Courage
Unchained	73	Visions of Friendship

Innervisions		
Poem Titles	**Page**	**Topic**
Unchain Me	86	Visions of Strength and Courage
Unforgettable	61	Visions of Life
Unselfishness	17	Visions of Nature
Utopia	32	Visions of Heaven
Values	72	Visions of Friendship
Visions	131	Visions of Peace
Weep No More	115	Visions of Love
Why Not Care	139	Visions of Peace
Yester Years	55	Visions of Life

About the Author

Calvin was born in Johns, Alabama. He was the third of seven children. His father worked the Alabama coal mines while his mother stayed home and tended to the children. He knew, growing up, that he wanted a better life for himself and in order to achieve his goals, he knew he had to leave home. As soon as he graduated from high school, he joined the U.S. Army where he remained a soldier for twenty years. During his active duty service, he traveled the world to include two tours of duty in war torn Vietnam. He was blessed to return home safely and promised himself to better his education. With the help of the GI Bill and years of hard work, he obtained a Master's Degree from Golden Gate University. After his military service, he went on to work as a US Government civilian and contractor, serving a total of fifty-nine years with the Department of the Army.

He started writing poetry at the age of twelve. He was sitting in the yard and noticed a robin in the maple tree feeding her babies—the sight of this lovely mother bird inspired him to begin writing poetry. He has always enjoyed writing and music, singing in the church choir as a boy, then professionally for over twenty years. His many life experiences gave him the strength, courage and compassion to be all that he can be and to serve his God, his country and his community.

CPSIA information can be obtained
at www.ICGtesting.com
Printed in the USA
FSHW020930151119
64078FS

9 781098 006716